PHOTOGRAPHING MESA VERDE

NORDENSKIÖLD AND NOW

By
William G. Howard
Douglas J. Hamilton
Kathleen L. Howard

D1707679

ISBN 1-887805-22-2

Authors
William G. Howard
Douglas J. Hamilton
Kathleen L. Howard

Mesa Verde Centennial Series Editor
Andrew Gulliford

Content and Copy Editor
Elizabeth A. Green

Design and Layout
Lisa Snider Atchison

Mesa Verde Centennial Series Editorial Committee
Lisa Snider Atchison, Tracey L. Chavis,
Elizabeth A. Green, Andrew Gulliford, Tessy Shirakawa,
Duane A. Smith and Robert Whitson

Printed in Korea

Memories of Mesa Verde

Watercolor by Shirley M. Hamilton

This book is dedicated to Shirley M. Hamilton:

wonderful wife, mother, teacher, artist, friend.

A message from the Superintendent
of Mesa Verde National Park

Our centennial celebrates an important moment in Mesa Verde National Park's history. It is an opportunity to share stories of what led to establishment of the park on June 29, 1906, and its designation as a World Heritage Cultural Site in 1978. This is a time to reflect upon its past and share hopes and visions for the next 100 years.

As Mesa Verde National Park nears its 100th birthday, it is important to remember that the archaeological sites it protects have been here far longer. Their survival is a credit to the skilled Ancestral Puebloan masons who created them 700 to 1600 years ago.

Following the Puebloan people's migration south to the Rio Grande area around 1300, the Utes continued to occupy the Mesa Verde area. They remain today and were responsible for the protection and preservation of Mesa Verde prior to its establishment as a national park. The park and the American public owe much to all these surviving indigenous people.

More than 100 years before its establishment as a national park, non-native people began exploring and documenting the archaeological sites at Mesa Verde, including Spanish explorers, geologists, ranchers, miners, photographers, naturalists, and archaeologists. They shared the story of fantastic stone cities in the cliffs, attracting more and more visitors to the area.

Prior to 1914, the 25-mile trek from Mancos Canyon to Spruce Tree House took an entire day, traveling the first 15 miles by wagon and the next 10 miles on foot or by horseback. This included a nearly vertical climb to the top of Chapin Mesa. Today more than one-half million people visit Mesa Verde National Park each year – a considerable increase over the 100 visitors documented in 1906.

"Leaving the past in place" is just one of the unique ideas pioneered at Mesa Verde. In 1908, when archaeology mainly consisted of collecting artifacts for distant museums, Jesse Walter Fewkes repaired, but did not rebuild, Spruce Tree House for visitation. He documented the excavation and created a small museum to house its artifacts. That tradition is continued today and Mesa Verde is recognized worldwide as a leader in non-invasive archaeology – studying and documenting sites without shovels to disturb the past. With the involvement of the 24 tribes affiliated with Mesa Verde and ongoing research, we continue to learn more about the stories that Mesa Verde National Park preserves.

Our centennial will celebrate 100 years of preservation and honor all who have gone before us. This centennial book series was created to tell some of their stories, of discovery, travel, transportation, archaeology, fire and tourism. These stories have contributed to our national heritage and reinforce why we must continue to preserve and protect this national treasure for future generations.

Enjoy the celebration. Enjoy the book series. Enjoy your national park.

– Larry T. Wiese

About the Mesa Verde Museum Association

Mesa Verde Museum Association (MVMA) is a nonprofit, 501 (c) 3 organization, authorized by Congress, established in 1930, and incorporated in 1960. MVMA was the second "cooperating association" formed in the United States after the Yosemite Association. Since its inception, the museum association has provided information that enables visitors to more fully appreciate the cultural and natural resources in Mesa Verde National Park and the southwestern United States. Working under a memorandum of agreement with the National Park Service, the association assists and supports various research activities, interpretive and education programs, and visitor services at Mesa Verde National Park.

A Board of Directors sets policy and provides guidance for the association. An Executive Director assures mission goals are met, strengthens partnerships, and manages publishing, education, and membership program development. A small year-round staff of five, along with more than 15 seasonal employees, operates four sales outlets in Mesa Verde National Park and a bookstore in Cortez, Colorado. The association carries nearly 600 items, the majority of which are produced by outside vendors. MVMA currently publishes approximately 40 books, videos, and theme-related items, and more than 15 trail guides.

Since 1996 MVMA has been a charter partner in the Plateau Journal, a semi-annual interpretive journal covering the people and places of the Colorado Plateau. In addition, the association has been a driving force in the Peaks, Plateaus & Canyons Association (PPCA), a region-wide conference of nonprofit interpretive associations. PPCA promotes understanding and protection of the Colorado Plateau through the publication of joint projects that are not feasible for smaller associations.

Mesa Verde Museum Association is also a longtime member of the Association of Partners for Public Lands (APPL). This national organization of nonprofit interpretive associations provides national representation with our land management partners and highly specialized training opportunities for board and staff.

Since 1930 the association has donated more than $2 million in cash contributions, interpretive services, and educational material to Mesa Verde National Park. MVMA's goal is to continue enhancing visitor experience through its products and services, supporting vital park programs in interpretation, research and education.

Visit the online bookstore at mesaverde.org and learn more about Mesa Verde National Park's centennial celebration at mesaverde2006.org. Contact MVMA offices for additional information at: telephone 970-529-4445; write P.O. Box 38, Mesa Verde National Park, CO 81330; or email info@mesaverde.org.

The Center of Southwest Studies

The Center of Southwest Studies on the campus of Fort Lewis College in Durango, Colorado, serves as a museum and a research facility, hosts public programs, and strengthens an interdisciplinary Southwest college curriculum. Fort Lewis College offers a four-year degree in Southwest Studies with minors in Native American Studies and Heritage Preservation. The Center includes a 4,400-square-foot gallery, the Robert Delaney Research Library, a 100-seat lyceum, and more than 10,000 square feet of collections storage. The new $8 million Center of Southwest Studies building is unique among four-year public colleges in the West, because the facility houses the departments of Southwest Studies and Anthropology, and the Office of Community Services, which helps Four Corners communities with historic preservation and cultural resource planning.

The Colorado Commission on Higher Education has recognized the Center of Southwest Studies as a "program of excellence" in state-funded higher education. Recent gifts to the Center include the $2.5 million Durango Collection ®, which features more than eight hundred years of southwestern weavings from Pueblo, Navajo and Hispanic cultures.

The goal of the Center is to become the intellectual heart of Durango and the Southwest and to provide a variety of educational and research opportunities for students, residents, scholars and visitors. Strengths in the Center's collections of artifacts include Ancestral Puebloan ceramic vessels, more than 500 textiles and dozens of southwestern baskets. The Center's holdings, which focus on the Four Corners region, include more than 8,000 artifacts, 20,000 volumes, numerous periodicals, and 500 special collections dating from prehistory to the present and with an emphasis on southwestern archaeology, maps, and original documents. These collections include nearly two linear miles of manuscripts, unbound printed materials, more than 7,000 rolls of microfilm (including about 3,000 rolls of historic Southwest region newspapers), 600 oral histories, and 200,000 photographs. Contact the Center at 970-247-7456 or visit the Center's website at swcenter.fortlewis.edu. The Center hosts tours, educational programs, a speakers' series, and changing exhibits throughout the year.

Center of SW Studies website: http://swcenter.fortlewis.edu

About the publisher

The publisher for the Mesa Verde Centennial Series is the Ballantine family of Durango and the Durango Herald Small Press. The Ballantine family moved to the Four Corners region in 1952 when they purchased the *Durango Herald* newspaper.

Durango has a magnificent setting, close to the Continental Divide, the 13,000-foot San Juan Mountains, and the 500,000-acre Weminuche Wilderness. The Four Corners region encompasses the juncture of Colorado, Utah, Arizona, and New Mexico, the only place in the nation where four state borders meet. Residents can choose to ski one day in the San Juans and hike the next day in the wilderness canyons of southeast Utah. This land of mountains and canyons, deserts and rivers is home to diverse Native American tribes including the Southern Utes, Ute Mountain Utes, Jicarilla Apache, Hopi, Zuni, and the Navajo, whose 17-million-acre nation sprawls across all four states. The Four Corners is situated on the edge of the Colorado Plateau, which has more national forests, national parks, national monuments, and wilderness areas than anywhere else on earth.

Writing and editing the newspaper launched countless family expeditions to Ancestral Puebloan sites in the area, including spectacular Mesa Verde National Park, the world's first park set aside for the preservation of cultural resources in 1906 to honor America's indigenous peoples. The Ballantine family, through the *Durango Herald* and the *Cortez Journal,* have been strong supporters of Mesa Verde National Park and Fort Lewis College.

Arthur and Morley Ballantine started the planning for the Center of Southwest Studies at Fort Lewis College in 1964 with a $10,000 gift. In 1994 Morley began the Durango Herald Small Press, which publishes books of local and regional interest. The Press is proud to be a part of the 100th birthday celebration for Mesa Verde National Park.

Durango Herald Small Press website: www.durangoheraldsmallpress.com

TABLE OF CONTENTS

**Our 1991 photography team from left:
Bill Howard, Kathy Howard, Doug Hamilton and Shirley Hamilton.**

PREFACE

Archival photographs are always intriguing: They provide windows on bygone times. The viewer wonders if the scenes still exist and how they have changed. In 1986, these questions occurred to me as I looked through Gustaf Nordenskiöld's 1891 pioneer photographs. Comparing today's Mesa Verde views with those of a century ago, I thought, might give clues to what sites, ecology, and landforms were like 700 years ago when prehistoric people lived at Mesa Verde. Re-photographing Nordenskiöld's scenes would be informative and focus attention on the signal contributions of Gustaf Nordenskiöld to Mesa Verde as well. My wife Kathy and I proposed the idea to Doug and Shirley Hamilton. Kathy is an historian and Shirley was a teacher and artist. Doug and I have electrical engineering backgrounds; we had been co-authors of an engineering textbook. All four of us had made many trips exploring the backcountry of Utah, Arizona, and Colorado.

We agreed that re-photographing Nordenskiöld's original work could be interesting, useful, and fun. I discussed the project with Mesa Verde National Park's then-chief of interpretation, Don Fiero, who suggested that it fit well with the Volunteer-In-Park (VIP) program. After assembling proposal and project plans, the four of us presented the project to then-

Superintendent Robert Heyder, who approved it. Over the succeeding several years our team traveled often to Mesa Verde National Park.

We chose to use a camera similar to Nordenskiöld's, and as a consequence spent many hours carrying bulky equipment over rough, precipitous terrain seeking sites and Nordenskiöld camera locations. Doug and I then spent hours in the park's darkroom developing and printing the results of our work. While darkroom activities were underway, Kathy researched Nordenskiöld's visit to Colroado and the Wetherill family's interaction with him. At the National Archives, and the Durango and Denver public libraries, she found much about Nordenskiöld's background and his legal difficulties.

By 1990 our team had finished the re-photographing and research phase of the project and selected photograph pairs that would form an interesting exhibit. Vic Goodwin, proprietor of Vic's Photos in Cortez, enlarged, printed, and mounted both the team's and Nordenskiöld's photographs. Park carpenters fabricated seven free-standing panels, and the team mounted the photographs and captions on them. The Spruce Tree Museum provided display space, and the exhibit, *A Century's Perspective: Gustaf Nordenskiöld's Mesa Verde Today*, opened in time for the park's Nordenskiöld Centennial Celebration in 1991. The exhibit was popular and was viewed by several hundred thousand museum visitors during the years it was in place. It finally became shopworn and was dismantled.

This book provides a lasting record of Mesa Verde's stability and change. Reaction to the original exhibit demonstrated substantial public interest in Mesa Verde's historic past – this book is written to help inform that interest.

– William G. Howard

I

MESA VERDE,
THE WETHERILLS
AND GUSTAF NORDENSKIÖLD

T he Mesa Verde is an intriguing island, a vast network of sloping mesas and deep canyons that stand above the surrounding landscape. It contains remnants of ancient peoples: basket makers and puebloans who flourished there for many generations, only to precipitously move away.

It is not known what events prompted them, after ages of hunting and gathering, to settle on the mesa tops, embrace agriculture and develop a complex spiritual culture. Nor is it clear what prompted them to move from the mesa tops down into alcoves in the steep canyon walls, where they built multi-storied structures of dressed stone – only to leave it all behind less than a century later. Despite 115 years of scientific investigation and countless theories, the answers to important questions remain speculative, based on the bits and pieces of material culture left behind as well as the beliefs and lifestyles of their descendants, the Pueblo people of New Mexico and Arizona.

The quest to tease as much understanding as possible from the sparse clues left by the ancient Mesa Verdeans has to be one of the great detective challenges of all time. Unlike other ancient civilizations, the Mesa Verde people left behind no Rosetta stone, no Sumerian accounts of commerce, and no sagas like the *Aeneid* or the Old Testament to guide archaeological investigation. What remains are isolated sites throughout the Four Corners area – monumental structures and piles of rubble with occasional pottery, weavings, and other piecemeal evidence to reconstruct nearly 1,500 years of life, culture, and struggle by extremely resourceful people to exist in what is today a harsh landscape. Modern Pueblo Indians provide some understanding of them through their oral traditions and clan symbols that persist from the times of their ancestors.

Local Ute Indians long knew of ancient cities on Colorado's Mesa Verde, but left the sites largely undisturbed for nearly 700 years. They considered the sites "Houses of the Dead" – disturbing them was taboo. Spanish explorers missed this prehistoric legacy entirely. An inscription in Bone Awl House reads, "T. Stangl, 1861." Who he was or what brought him there is, like so much else about Mesa Verde, open to speculation. In 1874 and 1876, members of two Hayden Survey parties found and cursorily excavated sites in and near Mancos Canyon, but even these well-equipped, sophisticated explorers passed by evidence of one of the most remarkable developments of North American prehistory in the rugged, inaccessible mesa country of Southwest Colorado. All too soon, however, sites in what was destined to become Mesa Verde National Park became endangered.

From the 1860s on, a small but growing number of people located, explored, and sometimes plundered dwellings located along canyons of the Mancos River and its tributaries. In the 1880s, a ranching family from Mancos began guiding visitors into the canyons, analyzing and taking notes as they excavated the abandoned cliff villages in an effort to learn

Gustaf Nils Adolph Nordenskiöld

about the people who had once inhabited them. Aided by Acowitz, a Ute companion, the Wetherill brothers and Charlie Mason, their sister Anna's husband, thoroughly explored the Mesa Verde. Working for other explorers, they removed artifacts that were sold to the Colorado Historical Society and later gathered a larger collection for another sponsor. At that time there was no Antiquities Act; such enterprises were entirely legal.

Mesa Verde National Park

Acowitz

Although the Wetherills and Mason lacked archaeological training and collected artifacts for sale to private collectors and museums, they developed an interest in the science of excavation. Gustaf Nordenskiöld was fortunate he hired the Wetherills to guide him into the canyon country of the Mesa Verde. Providentially, the young man from Sweden had scientific training and interest in exploring the sites. It was a visit that would have profound impact on Mesa Verde, according to Robert Heyder, superintendent of Mesa Verde National Park in 1984, who wrote, "I shudder to think what Mesa Verde would be today had there been no Gustaf Nordenskiöld. It is through his book that the notoriety of the cliff dwellings of Mesa Verde became known."

Gustaf Nils Adolph Nordenskiöld was born in Stockholm, Sweden, on June 29, 1868. His father, Nils Adolf Erik Nordenskiöld, was a baron, well-known scientist, arctic explorer, and chief of the mineralogical department of the Swedish Royal Academy of Science. Indeed, members of the Nordenskiöld family had, for many generations, been scientists and Gustaf was no exception. As a teenager he sailed the Baltic Sea, exploring its islands, and researched parts of Sweden, collecting plants, insects, and butterflies. In 1887 he enrolled at the University of Uppsala, completing his B.A. degree in three years. He then accompanied an expedition to explore and obtain scientific data on the arctic island of Spitsbergen. During this two-month expedition he contracted tuberculosis; his health so deteriorated that upon returning from Spitsbergen his father took him to Germany for treatment.

After a three-month stay in a Berlin clinic, Gustaf decided to travel the world to regain his health in warmer regions. Accordingly, in February 1891 he traveled to Munich, then on to Florence, Rome, Naples, the Isle of Capri, Marseilles, Paris, and New York. He found New York "an extremely noisy and dirty town, rather better some distance from the centre." From New York he journeyed to New Haven, Niagara, Charleston, Mammoth Cave, Chicago, and Denver. His goal was to visit museums and his itinerary was so planned.

How fortunate we are today that while browsing in the Denver Public Library in 1891, Gustaf Nordenskiöld met Alice Eastwood! A botanist who knew of sites at Mesa Verde, Miss Eastwood had been there with the Wetherills. She suggested he visit the sites and gave him letters of introduction to people in Durango and Mancos. Gustaf wrote to his family, "I have now also a ticket down to Durango in south Colorado and back here again. I am going there to look at the cliff dwellers."

From Durango Gustaf proceeded to the Wetherills' Alamo Ranch at Mancos. There he hired the Wetherill brothers to furnish equipment and act as guides so he could spend several days getting an overview of the Mesa Verde area and some sites. Planning only to take a quick look, he spent several days scouting in canyons and on mesa tops. He returned to the ranch so excited by what he had seen that he decided to take photographs and excavate some sites. That brief trip was to have a profound influence on Gustaf, the Wetherills, and Mesa Verde. Al Wetherill later recalled, "When he returned to the ranch his enthusiasm had increased almost beyond his control."

Again, Gustaf wrote to his family in mid-July.

> My intention was to stay about a week in Mancos Canyon. Now that week is gone, and I have made up my mind to stay for one or two months.
> ... before I determined upon the more extensive researches and excavations required to gain a thorough knowledge of the cliff-villages and their former inhabitants, I wished to undertake some preliminary work on a smaller scale.

Planning to excavate and photograph the sites, he asked his parents to send his camera equipment, explaining, "There is no series of photographs in existence of these remarkable ruins."

Gustaf's father was less than enthusiastic about the Mesa Verde adventure. He wrote several letters to his son, imploring him "not to forget geology and mineralogy" and suggesting that he come home to lead a South Pole expedition. But Gustaf persisted, spending four months (July through October 1891) at Mesa Verde. He spent most of this time excavating sites and selecting specimens for shipment to Sweden, where he hoped they would be put on display. During the last weeks he did extensive photographic documenting of what he had found. The result was a collection of about 150 black-and-white photographs.

MESA VERDE TODAY

Mesa Verde National Park has a long tradition of providing public access to sites. When scientists excavate a site, they carefully preserve archaeological remains for study and interpretation. They then stabilize the site to ensure structural integrity and to arrest deterioration. They also make any necessary safety modifications. Visitors today can see many of the sites visited by Gustaf Nordenskiöld – reminders of the ancient people that lived here at the time Europe was experiencing the Middle Ages.

Of course, not all sites can be opened to public access. Some are too difficult to reach or too fragile, and only a few are of great interest to the majority of visitors. Yet excavation of these sites adds much to our understanding of prehistoric life and times. So far the National Park Service has excavated and stabilized 94 sites.

2

PHOTOGRAPHS
AND PHOTOGRAPHERS

Photographer Doug Hamilton in a ruin at Mesa Verde National Park.

G ustaf Nordenskiöld played a critical role in the establishment and development of Mesa Verde National Park. Others were also key: Acowitz and the Wetherills, who disclosed the secrets of the Mesa to the world; Jesse Walter Fewkes and Jesse Nusbaum, early archaeologists at the park; Virginia McClurg and Lucy Peabody, of the Colorado Cliff Dwellings Association; and many more who fought for the park's designation and contributed to its preservation and distinction. But Nordenskiöld was special; he arrived on the scene at a time when enough of the cliff dwellings remained intact that he was able to learn something of their builders and occupants.

As a tourist, Gustaf could have observed the sites, scribbled on their walls, gathered up relics and hurried on to the next attraction in the West. That was his initial plan. Instead, he became spellbound by the area. He fell prey to his curiosity and stayed to study further. He resorted to the skills and techniques he had learned as a geologist and educated scientist to try to make sense of the jumble of rocks, walls, and artifacts that littered the alcoves. By carefully observing location and relationships between objects and structures, keeping records, making sketches, deducing the passage of time through strata, and hypothesizing about the past, Gustaf practiced the rudiments of archaeological fieldwork; by his example he taught the Wetherills. He reinforced in them the opportunities to learn from cultural remnants and the need for care in handling such evidence of prehistory.

Nordenskiöld was an amateur at archaeology, but most archaeologists of his day were, too, as they sought to develop and improve the tools and tech-

Bill Howard photographing at Step House.

niques of their new science. Gustaf's relic collection ended up in Helsinki, where it is cared for by the National Museum of Finland. He published the results of his work in *Cliff Dwellers of the Mesa Verde* and exhibited more than 110 photographs and relics in the *Exposición Histórica-Americana* at the Columbian Historical Exposition in Madrid in 1892-93.

Counterparts to the Spanish exhibition could be viewed in Chicago at the World's Columbian Exposition of 1893 where two collections from Mesa Verde were displayed. One was in the Anthropology Building and the other on the Pike, the "main street" of the exposition. Visitors to the White City's Pike could study the *Cliff Dwellers Exhibit* and see facsimile *estufas* (now known as kivas) and reproductions of Balcony House and Cliff Palace. Prehistoric relics from Mesa Verde were also on display.

In terms of impact, *Cliff Dwellers of the Mesa Verde* stands out. Clearly, Gustaf had exceptional talent for field observation, but he went further by documenting his findings, developing theories and publishing them. *Cliff Dwellers* is a remarkable work. Based on only four months of direct observation, it clearly demonstrates Nordenskiöld's brilliance. The book has remained in print from its initial publication to today. Thousands of readers have learned about the prehistoric Southwest through the Swedish scientist's eyes.

Above: Nordenskiöld's mark in Painted Kiva House. Notice the "W" for Wetherill.
Below top: Site 6 in Pool Canyon. Below bottom: Jug House.

Nordenskiöld's photographs are important elements in documenting his observations. They provide a comprehensive, early record of the Mesa Verde sites and the surrounding area. They show sites in a condition close to what it was at the time the Wetherills came upon them. The photographs provide a baseline against which to assess the effects of extensive stabilization and modifications to accommodate large numbers of visitors in developed sites, and the effects of the passage of time in those that have been left alone. His pictures document much more than just sites – they portray the relatively isolated world of the Mesa Verde in 1891.

Nordenskiöld and the Wetherills covered the major cliff sites well. In each site he visited, he inscribed a number to identify the site and to index it to his other field observations. Even today, each site he visited bears a "Nordenskiöld number" to testify to his presence.

Nordenskiöld was well-equipped for

Mesa Verde National Park/Gustaf Nordenskiöld

The Wetherills lowering Nordenskiöld's gear to Little Long House in 1891.

Bill Howard

Doug Hamilton lowers himself down the same crevasse.

Little Long House foils Wetherill "cliff lizards."

photography from his earlier scientific fieldwork; he had the skill to portray his subject well. His photos are clear, well formatted, and illustrate the salient points of his Mesa Verde experience.

We sought to duplicate, as closely as possible, Nordenskiöld's images a century after he took them. We used, for the most part, a 4-inch-by-5-inch view camera to simulate Gustaf's large format equipment. The film he used had very high contrast that did not reveal details in shadows and brightly lit areas; we used modern film with a more extended contrast range capable of reproducing more features in a scene.

We took our photographs as close as feasible to the camera location for the Nordenskiöld originals. However, bushes, trees, and changes in land-form sometimes made original locations unreachable.

Whereas young Nordenskiöld had the Wetherills to guide and support him, our middle-aged party of four relied on the assistance of the National Park Service and the Ute Mountain Ute Indian Tribe. Their research resources and knowledge of the area made our visits to Mesa Verde much easier than Nordenskiöld's. Their hospitality and support were all we could have asked for.

Access to Mesa Verde's isolated sites can be difficult. Reaching them over the cliffs and along ledges, with camera, excavating and camping equipment was challenging.

Although the Wetherills were evidently part mountain goat, even they encountered structures that defied their propensity for high places. Without technical climbing gear, for example, we could not reach even the camera position from which Nordenskiöld photographed Little Long House.

PHOTO COMPARISON

Comparing and contrasting Gustaf Nordenskiöld's 1891 photographs with our more recent pictures reveals a great deal about stability and change in Mesa Verde's cliff sites. The juxtaposition also indicates how the Mesa environment – its plant life and landforms – have changed.

The effect of change in many sites is a result of archaeological excavation and National Park Service stabilization and adaptations for public visitors. Other sites remain essentially as they were found by Nordenskiöld and the Wetherills, with minor stabilization. They await some future time when techniques of both analysis and stabilization, as well as budget and access, may permit further study.

After examining the 1991 images together with those taken in 1891, we came to the conclusion that today's Mesa is very overgrown compared to that of a century earlier. Photos of sites, check dams, overlooks, and ranches all indicated a landscape where trees, bushes, and other plants have thrived. We attributed the overgrowth to the zeal of the park service in dousing large fires. We also concluded that Mesa Verde is an environment where changes occur very slowly. Except for a few isolated rock falls, the mesa scene is little disturbed by a hundred years of aging in the relatively dry climate (see Chapter 6). Check dam rocks and tree limbs photographed in 1891 appeared in the same place in 1991. Some of the yucca plants alive in Nordenskiöld's time have survived a hundred years.

Then came five major fires between 1996 and 2003. When we re-visited Mesa Verde in the summer of 2005 to finish research activities, we found the landscape completely changed. Scrub oaks that had blanketed the park were burned to the ground. Trees were reduced to skeletons, and the ground cover was dominated by thistles that spring up in the wake of fires. The effects of erosion have greatly increased and rocks that were previously unmoved since Nordenskiöld's time are no longer to be found close by.

Clearly, change at Mesa Verde takes place in infrequent giant steps, separated by long periods of creeping shift. We have not yet been able to return to those sites that would most clearly chronicle change since 1991 and to compare them to what took place in the previous century.

Pictures shown in the remainder of this book consist mostly of photo pairs, one from Nordenskiöld's collection, the other taken by our team 100 years later. They are presented on facing pages to facilitate scrutiny of similarities and differences. As much as practical, the 20th century photos are taken from the same place as the 19th century views; however, it was not always possible to match the time and date.

3

NORDENSKIÖLD'S
MESA VERDE EXPERIENCE

H ow interesting it would have been to be at the Wetherills' Alamo Ranch when Gustaf Nordenskiöld arrived on July 2, 1891! Here was a meeting of people from two widely disparate backgrounds, and, although none of those involved could know it, the beginning of a lasting friendship. The visitor was a tall, slender young man with a university degree, doubtless of aristocratic bearing, from a privileged family in Sweden, looking for something to do. In contrast, the Wetherills were a hard-working family struggling to survive by hardscrabble ranching and guiding.

The family patriarch, Benjamin Wetherill, and his wife Marian, were Quakers who migrated from Pennsylvania with their six children – five boys and a girl. After farming in Kansas and mining in Missouri, Benjamin acquired a homestead site near Mancos, Colorado, and the family joined him there in 1881. They constructed a log cabin and established the Alamo Ranch. In 1882, Al located and explored an ancient site. More site discoveries followed, leading to more extensive explorations. John, Richard, and Al became preoccupied with prehistoric Indian sites – a fascination that dominated the rest of their lives.

By 1887, a scattering of people had visited the ranch, hiring the Wetherills to show them the sites. The Wetherills continued to explore, and in 1888 were hired to gather artifacts for a collection that was sold to the Colorado State Historical Society. During the next few years the number of tourists increased, and by the time Gustaf arrived on July 2, 1891, the Alamo Ranch guest register contained names from as far away as Pennsylvania and Connecticut.

The name Nordenskiöld was familiar to the Wetherills; they had heard of Gustaf's father's Arctic voyage in the *Vega*, and his discovery of a northeast passage to the Orient. Nevertheless, it is likely that their initial impression was that 23-year-old Gustaf was just another wealthy curiosity-seeking tourist referred to them by their friend Alice Eastwood.

On July 11, 1891, Gustaf wrote to his parents of his arrival at Alamo Ranch.

> I mentioned in my last letter that I was going to southwestern Colorado to see the so-called cliff dwellings in Mancos Canyon. I went by train to Durango and from there by coach to Mancos. There I stayed with a farmer named Wetherill, who drives his cattle in the tract where the cliff dwellings are, and thus knows them well. He himself is old, and stays at home while the boys drive the cattle down into the valley. I decided to go with them to a place where they camp, and then go with one of them to visit the ruins.

When Gustaf had met Alice Eastwood in Denver, she certainly would have given him a detailed description of what was to be seen with the Wetherills, who had guided her to sites in 1890. However, even this could not have prepared him for the breathtaking and awe-inspiring sights he

The Wetherill brothers from left: Al, Winslow, Richard, Clayton and John

would see. Mesa Verde captured his interest as nothing else had on his long journey. A week's stay quickly grew into months.

In reading the description of his initial trip to the sites, one cannot help but be impressed with the strenuousness of the trip and the rigors he was subjected to, particularly in view of his poor health. Nordenskiöld spent the last two days of the week at a small cliff dwelling of 11 rooms, where he and his two guides did much digging and "found a number of things." He then returned to Mancos.

By now Gustaf had become enthralled by the scope and condition of the cliff dwellings. Al Wetherill noted that,

> His idea then was to get an outfit in shape and go to work to find some clue as to the who, the what and the where of the lost people."
> Finding that we lacked outside support in what we were doing, he expressed a wish to make a collection that would be on permanent public exhibit in Sweden. He was so taken up with the subject that he had us get an outfit together for further exploration and excavation.

Mesa Verde National Park

Gustaf in his camping attire.

Clearly, Nordenskiöld was hooked.

With some of the Wetherills as guides, laborers, and companions, Gustaf now began what was to become an almost four-month odyssey of exploration, excavation, and photography. Wisely, he realized that before undertaking full-scale large site excavations, he needed first to investigate a small site in order to learn what he might encounter. Richard Wetherill advised him to begin in the site the Wetherills had named No. 9, which later became known as Painted Kiva House. Next, Gustaf and his party excavated Long House, because he thought this "was the most favorable for quick results."

Typically, the budding archaeologists camped near sites, and spent the daylight hours excavating and cataloging. Occasionally the party took advantage of the shelter provided by a site. Excavating was hard, dusty work; in later explorations Al wrote of "all the mummy dust we ate while we dug through those hot summer days." Gustaf took a few photographs, but had only a small Kodak camera; his more sophisticated camera equipment did not arrive from Sweden until most of the excavations were finished. The group made frequent trips to the ranch for supplies, and sometimes even to Durango to obtain permits for crossing or working on Ute lands, and to arrange for shipment of artifacts.

Gustaf was apparently a parsimonious employer. In later years Al commented, "While working in the sites, Nordenskiöld would mumble to himself that he had to 'pay more for help around here in a month' than he would have to pay in his country in a year and that he was paying John as much per day as a professor earned in Sweden. All that, though, fell on deaf and silent ears, so far as we were concerned."

In camp, one of the Wetherills, usually Al, did the cooking. That Nordenskiöld enjoyed some humor at his own expense is shown by his observations of his own ineptitude as a camp cook:

> I sent Al to fetch provisions the next morning, and had nothing to do but kill time as best I could. I went with Al for a little way, and it was nearly midday when I got back to the camp. I was now faced with a difficult problem. Al, my incomparable cook, was gone. Where was my dinner coming from? My hunger convinced me of the necessity of cooking for myself. Our stock of provisions was small, as was my experience cooking for myself. It being necessary to take both these things into consideration, I decided on the following bill of fare, porridge without salt, tea without sugar, bread without yeast. Our cooking utensils were the simplest possible: coffee pot and frying pan plus empty tin cans. The frying pan also served for baking. Baking the bread was the most difficult problem, so I started with that. I mixed flour and water and other ingredients that I had seen Al use, got flour and dough up to my

Dinner is served.
From left: John Wetherill and Al Wetherill in Spruce Tree House.

elbows, on my nose and everywhere else. The lump of dough was put into the frying pan and placed on the fire until it had turned blackish-brown. In the meantime the tea and porridge were boiled. The latter, however, was nothing but a mixture of oats and water.

Everything was ready. "Dinner was served," and I was just going to begin eating with a real camp appetite, when I heard the sound of horses. Two dark complexioned youths on small, high-mettled ponies came galloping into camp. They jumped quickly out of their saddles, sat down and made themselves at home. My guests were Indians. Their clothes were half civilized, their hair long and straight, hung down over their shoulders and hit part of their faces. One of them, a young boy, had an uncommonly fine and pleasant face, regular features and large dark eyes. I wished to show my guests hospitality, but felt little inclined to sacrifice my dinner, which had caused me so much trouble to prepare.

After much searching among saddles, blankets, bridles, saddle bags, lassos, etc. that lay in a heap under a bush, I found a bundle of cigarettes, which I offered the red skins. They accepted with delight. I thought I had satisfied them, and hoped they would go and let me begin my already cold dinner. But no. They showed no desire to go, but threw longing glances toward the brown product from the frying pan which was supposed to be bread. With a sigh I decided to sacrifice my dinner. I made a gesture with my hand to the piece of sail-cloth on which all my dainties were laid. My friends the redskins nodded and began eating at once. The bread and the tea without sugar disappeared quickly, but the porridge was too much for them.

Nordenskiöld had journeyed to Alamo Ranch at an ideal time for both himself and the Wetherills. The ranchers had identified and named all of the major cliff dwellings, compiled collections of artifacts, and guided tourists to the sites. They were thus able to help Gustaf determine how best to spend his time excavating and photographing. The collections they had made enabled them to give him some details of what to expect. However, their knowledge of archaeological techniques was entirely self-taught. They had sought guidance from the Smithsonian without success. Now they had someone who was willing to teach them more about scientific methods of excavation and record-keeping. The science of archaeology was in its infancy, and the methods Nordenskiöld and the Wetherills used were on a par with what was then state of the art.

Gustaf, on the other hand, needed guides to take him to the sites, to provide labor for excavation, to supply pack animals, and to do the cooking. For his part, he was able to provide needed scientific expertise. He was familiar with the use of stratigraphy – the study of strata, or layers, in this instance the interpretation of soil and geological strata containing archaeological materials in order to determine the relative ages of layers – and he understood the importance of recording every artifact that was found, and its location, and of making detailed drawings of the floor plans of sites. He was also able to do the necessary photography. An astute observer, his careful examination of ceramics found in Step House led him to speculate that there had been two different occupations of that site. The Wetherills shared that conclusion based on other observations related to pottery at the site. Studies in later years proved them right.

Had Gustaf arrived just a few years later, the devastation of sites by pot hunters and curiosity seekers would have decimated what is now Mesa Verde National Park. Fortunately, the Wetherills were anxious to learn from him. Although none of those involved realized it at the time, a synergistic partnership had begun.

Gustaf remained at Mesa Verde and Alamo Ranch until November 4, 1891. He then made an extensive and difficult trip to the Grand Canyon with Al Wetherill and Roe Ethridge as guides, after which he returned to Sweden. He continued to correspond with the Wetherills until his untimely death in 1894.

4

NORDENSKIÖLD'S FIRST EXCAVATIONS

W hat began for Nordenskiöld as a sightseeing trip to the cliff dwellings of Southwest Colorado quickly became a scientific examination. Drawing on his past fieldwork training and advice from his guides, he selected a relatively small site for his first excavations, Painted Kiva House.

After working in Painted Kiva House, Nordenskiöld felt that he had enough experience to begin more extensive excavations. He was eager to assemble a collection of artifacts that would form a permanent public exhibit in Sweden. Consulting with the Wetherills, he decided Long House would be the cliff dwelling that would require the least excavation to yield the most artifacts, and chose it as the site for his first comprehensive investigations.

The Wetherills named Long House, and Al thought that "it may have surpassed Cliff Palace at one time but much of it lacks protection and so suffered from the elements."

Located far from the cluster of

Bill Howard

View across Spruce Tree House.

better known cliff dwellings and visitor facilities on Chapin Mesa, Long House received relatively little public attention in Mesa Verde's early years. After World War II, park visitation increased rapidly. In 1946 39,843 people visited Mesa Verde; by 1956 the number had more than quadrupled to 186,808. The fragile ruins of the most popular cliff dwellings – Cliff Palace, Spruce Tree House, and Balcony House – were suffering from the wear and tear of so many tourists.

To relieve the pressure, the National Park Service made plans to open sites on Wetherill Mesa, such as Long House, Step House, and older mesa top sites. In conjunction with the National Geographic Society, from 1958-1961, those sites were excavated and stabilized. Just as in the 1890s, access was a challenge. Road construction was difficult, but finally in 1973 the park service opened Long House to public access. Step House followed in 1974.

Painted Kiva House

1891

Mesa Verde National Park/Gustaf Nordenskiöld

"On the advice of Richard Wetherill I began this work in a ruin in Cliff Canon where only very little excavation had been carried out previously." Nordenskiöld spent two days excavating there and later returned to take photographs. The Wetherills had identified this as Site 9; it is now known as Painted Kiva House because of designs painted on the kiva wall.

Bill Howard

Jesse Walter Fewkes excavated and stabilized Painted Kiva House in 1921. The effects of his investigations and later reconstruction have changed the ruin's details but not its basic structures.

Mesa Verde National Park/Gustaf Nordenskiöld

In the kiva, Gustaf noted, "The lower part of the wall to a height of 0.4 metres is painted dark red around the whole room. This red paint projects upwards in triangular points, arranged in threes, and above them is a row of small round dots of red."

Bill Howard

Red paint is still visible today although the effects of rubble removal and reconstruction have changed the view in small ways. The triangle-and-dot pattern Nordenskiöld mentioned also appears in Cliff Palace and some other ruins.

LONG HOUSE

1891

Mesa Verde National Park/Gustaf Nordenskiöld

Having experienced difficulty gaining access to parts of the ruin, Gustaf noted, "we reach a wide, semicircular hollow, a kind of gigantic niche with high vaulted roof. Along the inner part thereof rises a row of partly fallen walls of mounds of sandstone blocks from which a blackened rafter projects here and there."

Bill Howard

Following extensive reconstruction and stabilization by national park personnel, Long House was opened to the public in 1973. The structures hidden under rubble in Nordenskiöld's time are now revealed.

Mesa Verde National Park/Gustaf Nordenskiöld

Nordenskiöld and his crew spent a long time digging at Long House with disappointing results. They worked there sporadically for about a month "without making many finds of special interest ... the walls were so often dilapidated, and the rooms so full of rubble and stones, that long labour was necessary to reach the floors where we might expect to find the most numerous objects." John Wetherill is seen here taking notes.

Bill Howard

Little has changed since Nordenskiöld's day, except that latter day archaeologists have cleared rubble from the site. The open area in back of Long House is still a cool, shady place to catch up on field notes.

5

The Cliff Dwellings

Mesa Verde National Park/Gustaf Nordenskiöld

A Wetherill scaling the ruins.

F rom late July until mid-October 1891, Nordenskiöld contin-ued excavating cliff dwellings. He made trips to Mancos for supplies, and to Durango to ship specimens. By mid-October he received his camera equipment and spent the last weeks of October primarily taking photographs of cliff dwellings.

Differences between today's photos and Nordenskiöld's are mainly the result of subsequent excavation and stabilization by the National Park Service (NPS). Cleared of rubble, sites' salient features are now more rec-ognizable; stabilization has arrested further deterioration. The care and dedication of the National Park Service to the protection of the sites, and to accuracy of interpretive material is impressive. Even with annual visita-tion surpassing 500,000 people, the NPS provides visitors a meaningful experience in many of the most significant sites.

In 1934 the park service recognized that it needed a consistent stabiliza-tion program to preserve sites that cannot be excavated. In Mesa Verde National Park there are nearly 600 Cliff Dweller sites with standing walls. A stabilization crew monitors these sites to determine which ones require preservation. Their oversight includes all sites: those open to the public as well as those that are closed. The size of the stabilization effort today is determined by available funds.

SPRUCE TREE HOUSE

1891

Mesa Verde National Park/Gustaf Nordenskiöld

In September of 1891, Nordenskiöld moved his camp to a branch of Navajo Canyon, where there was "a large cave, in the shadow of which lie the ruins of a whole village, Spruce Tree House." The Wetherills named it that because of a large tree growing in the ruins of a kiva. The namesake tree was actually a fir, and Gustaf did not hesitate to cut it down so that he could count the rings, hoping to obtain some information about the age of the dwelling. He tallied 167 rings, but could make no significant conclusions about the age of the dwelling. His effort foreshadowed the development of dendrochronology, one of the most widely used archaeological techniques for estimating age of southwestern prehistoric structures.

Bill Howard

In 1908, just two years after the creation of Mesa Verde National Park, Jesse Walter Fewkes excavated and stabilized Spruce Tree House. He cleared rubble from the Spruce Tree House plaza, and re-roofed and rebuilt some kivas before opening it to the public. An interesting historical footnote: In 1917 Virginia McClurg staged in Spruce Tree House a romantic and completely fictional pageant called, "The Marriage of the Dawn and the Moon." What would Nordenskiöld have thought of this?

Mesa Verde National Park/Gustaf Nordenskiöld

Nordenskiöld commented about Spruce Tree House:
"The walls and roof of some rooms are thick with soot. The inhabitants must have had no great pretension as regards light and air."

Bill Howard

An alcove protects Spruce Tree House from the effects of weather, making it one of the
best preserved sites at Mesa Verde.

Mesa Verde National Park/Gustaf Nordenskiöld

The structure at the north end of Spruce Tree House as it appeared to
Nordenskiöld, prior to excavation and stabilization.

Bill Howard

The same structure a century later. Even after excavation and stabilization, the appearance of some structures in Spruce Tree House is the same as in Nordenskiöld's time.

CLIFF PALACE

1891

Mesa Verde National Park/Gustaf Nordenskiöld

Richard Wetherill named Cliff Palace. When Nordenskiöld saw it he wrote, "This ruin well deserves its name, for with its round towers and high walls rising out of heaps of stones deep in the mysterious twilight of the cavern, and defying in their sheltered site the ravages of time, it resembles at a distance an enchanted castle."

Bill Howard

Cliff Palace is the most spectacular site at Mesa Verde today and still deserves to be called enchanted. Visitors now roam on paved paths where Nordenskiöld and the Wetherills had to scramble over rocks and rubble.

Mesa Verde National Park/Gustaf Nordenskiöld

"In a long but not very deep branch of Cliff Cañon, a wild and gloomy gorge named Cliff Palace Cañon, lies the largest of the sites on the Mesa Verde, the Cliff Palace. Strange and indescribable is the impression on the traveller [*sic*], when, after a long and tiring ride through the boundless, monotonous piñon forest, he suddenly halts on the brink of the precipice, and in the opposite cliff beholds the ruins of the Cliff Palace, framed in the massive vault of rock above and in a bed of sunlit cedar and piñon trees below."

Bill Howard

After Jesse Walter Fewkes completed his work in Spruce Tree House, he excavated and stabilized Cliff Palace in 1909. He reported that it was in good enough condition to be opened to the public, but that it had been thoroughly looted for commercial purposes and many of its relics were lost forever.

$$\boxed{1891}$$

Mesa Verde National Park/Gustaf Nordenskiöld

Kiva "D" in Cliff Palace. John Wetherill sits on the ledge. Note the names on the wall
include many early Mesa Verde visitors, including John's brother Clayton
and Alice Eastwood.

Bill Howard

Kiva "D" without John Wetherill. The graffiti was obliterated a few years after Nordenskiöld's visit, and the kiva has been cleaned up, but it remains basically the same.

BALCONY HOUSE

1891

Mesa Verde National Park/Gustaf Nordenskiöld

John Wetherill on the Balcony House "balcony." When Nordenskiöld mentioned Balcony House in his journal, he called it Brown Stone Front House. "The ruin 'Brown Stone Front House' has its name because the outer sides of several walls are painted with a red-brown paint, otherwise only used inside the houses." The skill of the builders impressed him: "This cliff dwelling is the best preserved of all the ruins on the Mesa Verde. It also seems as if the architecture of the cliff people had here reached its culminating point."

Bill Howard

John Wetherill has gone, but the balcony remains. Jesse Nusbaum excavated and stabilized Balcony House in 1910.

Mesa Verde National Park/Gustaf Nordenskiöld

Balcony House interior showing the original condition of the structures.

Bill Howard

Balcony House interior structures as cleaned up, repaired and stabilized by Jesse Nusbaum. Note the original extended beams have been straightened and the walls have been shored up with iron straps.

Mesa Verde National Park/Gustaf Nordenskiöld

In Nordenskiöld's day, this tunnel was the only way into or out of Balcony House, making it an extremely secure defensive position.

Bill Howard

Although visitors now climb a ladder to enter Balcony House, they still exit through the tunnel. The iron door has been added to protect the site from unsupervised visitors.

Kathy Howard

This door's small size illustrates the defensive strength of Balcony House.

SQUARE TOWER HOUSE

1891

The Wetherills claimed to have found coal ashes in Square Tower House. If true, this is the only instance in which prehistoric people in this area used coal as fuel. The claim is not too surprising, however, since coal deposits exist in the strata of Mesa Verde.

Bill Howard

Jesse Walter Fewkes excavated and stabilized Square Tower House in 1919 and opened it
to the public. The National Park Service did additional stabilization in 1934,
but closed the site in 1954.

Mesa Verde National Park

Nordenskiöld had great interest in kivas, then called *estufas* (Spanish for stoves). In Square Tower House he "crept into one of the estufas, the nearer to the cliff. The floor was covered with rubbish to a depth of several feet." Later he wrote, "On my way through the Navajo Reservation I observed a hogan – the name given by these Indians to a house – constructed in exactly the same manner as the roof of the estufa in Square Tower House, or of horizontal poles laid in a ring." This is the only photograph we have of Nordenskiöld in the field at Mesa Verde.

Bill Howard

Nordenskiöld had correctly deduced the structure of the prehistoric kiva. By resting logs on vertical pillars, or pilasters, the ancients were able to build large covered rooms without using pillars in the middle of the room or long logs. The diameter of the typical kiva is much greater than the length of the logs used in its construction. In this photo, Doug Hamilton contemplates Nordenskiöld's visit.

Spring House

Mesa Verde National Park/Gustaf Nordenskiöld

Spring House is one of the most interesting sites that has been stabilized but not excavated. It is so named because of a spring at the back of the cave. Nordenskiöld wrote, "What a striking view these ruins present at a distance! The explorer pictures to himself a whole town in miniature under the lofty vault of rock in the cliff before him. But the town is a deserted one: not a sound breaks the silence, and not a movement meets the eye, among those gloomy, half-ruined walls, whose contours stand off sharply from the darkness of the inner cave."

Bill Howard

Spring House is not open to the public. As we stood there, just the four of us, gazing in awe at the site sheltered by its alcove, we knew what Nordenskiöld and the Wetherills had experienced. The stillness of the buildings, frozen in time, and the silence were overwhelming. A gentle whisper of a breeze and the occasional raucous squawk of a raven echoing from the alcove walls accentuated the mystical aura that pervaded the scene. Although Spring House has not been excavated since Nordenskiöld's time, it was first stabilized in 1935. Note where the stabilization crew reinforced a wall to prevent its collapse.

Mesa Verde National Park/Gustaf Nordenskiöld

Spring House contains one remarkable feature seen in few other sites: a free-standing pillar to shore up an upper room's floor. This structural innovation is a reminder of the tools prehistoric Mesa Verdeans lacked – the wheel and a written language, to name two. In light of such limitations, their accomplishments are even more amazing.

Bill Howard

The pillar remains erect and the beams holding the upper room are still in place. The team found Spring House a most interesting site. There were several features there that we had not seen in other sites. On some walls the handprints of the makers were clearly visible. The National Park Service began limited stabilization of Spring House in 1935, 44 years after Nordenskiöld and the Wetherills explored it.

1891

Mesa Verde National Park/Gustaf Nordenskiöld

The Wetherills named this prominent structure overlooking Navajo Canyon the Navajo Watch Tower. Although it is not a cliff dwelling, it is interesting because it shows imaginative use of a naturally occurring rock point that lacks any protective shelter. The National Park Service has never excavated it.

Bill Howard

In the 75 years between Nordenskiöld's photo and its stabilization in 1966, Navajo Watch Tower changed little. For those who might wonder, balancing on the rock below the tower is a lot harder than it looks.

6

MESA VERDE'S NATURAL ENVIRONMENT

W hile Gustaf Nordenskiöld is best known for excavating and photographing sites, he also took pictures of scenes that show Mesa Verde's ecology and geology. The collection of his Mesa Verde photographs provides valuable information about changes that have occurred during the passing of a century. They also show some surprising instances where little change has taken place.

Intuitively, one would expect that the more sheltered cliff dwellings should withstand the relentless forces of nature better than those that are fully exposed. That is not

Bill Howard

Mesa Verde's mule deer population has flourished.

always the case. As Chapter 5 shows, Navajo Watch Tower is completely isolated and exposed, yet shows very little change from the time Nordenskiöld photographed it until it was stabilized in the 1960s. When Nordenskiöld photographed a check dam on the cliff above Kodak House, there was a fallen dead tree across it. A century later the fallen tree, with some of its branches still intact, was still in place. In contrast, some of the cliff dwellings, though located in alcoves, had many walls that had fallen. Other features were reduced to rubble.

Human impact has also changed since Nordenskiöld's time. Before Mesa Verde became a national park, little was done to manage the ecology. Local ranchers and Ute Indians grazed cattle throughout the area. This is no longer the case within the park boundary; as a result, vegetation is more abundant. Unfortunately, that abundance of plant life increases the potential for wildfires, as was shown with devastating effect between 1996 and 2003, when fires raged through nearly 60 percent of Mesa Verde National Park.

Humans have also had a benevolent impact in the stabilization work done by the park service to preserve the sites. Less than a century has elapsed since work was initiated in order to make the sites available to the general public, while at the same time preventing the sites from being degraded by the impact of hundreds of thousands of visitors.

Mesa Verde National Park/Gustaf Nordenskiöld

John Wetherill seated on a Navajo Canyon overlook. Mesa Verde has always been a great place to reflect on nature.

Doug Hamilton

Little has changed in Mesa Verde's overall appearance. Bill Howard found it is still a good place to rest and contemplate the scenery.

Mesa Verde National Park/Gustaf Nordenskiöld

This seemingly uninteresting photograph is perhaps the most remarkable one in the set. It shows the remains of a check dam, used by Ancestral Puebloans to trap runoff water. Located on the mesa top near Kodak House, it is completely exposed. Notice the large fallen tree across the dam.

Bill Howard

In the ensuing 100 years, rushing water has moved a few rocks, and some fallen trees are no longer present. The prominent one in Nordenskiöld's photograph is still there, as are two of its branches. Vegetation in the vicinity is now more abundant.

Mesa Verde National Park/Gustaf Nordenskiöld

In the canyon below Cliff Palace, Nordenskiöld and his friends found a shallow pool of water. John Wetherill posed on a rock above it.

Doug Hamilton

Because of its location we thought the pool might have been a water source used by the inhabitants, so we examined the area for traces of human use. Our efforts were rewarded when we found small steps cut into the cliff face. Following these steps up to the next ledge we ultimately found a faint trail leading to Cliff Palace.

Mesa Verde National Park/Gustaf Nordenskiöld

Nordenskiöld took this view of some small sites across the canyon from a trail leading to Tree House in what is now the Ute Mountain Tribal Park.

Bill Howard

Not only are the ruins still there, but remarkably, some of the same trees are present even after 100 years. Vegetation is now denser on the mesa top than in Nordenskiöld's time, as was generally the case everywhere.

Mesa Verde National Park/Gustaf Nordenskiöld

Nordenskiöld photographed these rock steps from which Step House gets its name.

Bill Howard

Here are the same steps today. They are completely exposed, and undergrowth is now much denser. Nevertheless, one can still identify individual rocks fitted in place by the original inhabitants.

Mesa Verde National Park/Gustaf Nordenskiöld

This Pool Canyon site is a great place for a room with a view. Notice the yucca plants in the foreground.

Bill Howard

A century later, yucca plants still grow from the same rhizomes.

Mesa Verde National Park/Gustaf Nordenskiöld

Compared to structural shifts in cliff dwellings, and to ecological changes, geo-
logic changes usually occur slowly, over thousands or even millions of years.
Nordenskiöld photographed these steps cut into the rock.

Bill Howard

The same steps show imperceptible change over a century of exposure to the elements.

Mesa Verde National Park/Gustaf Nordenskiöld

Nordenskiöld found two types of petroglyphs, "one of them closely resembling the picture writing of modern Indians, which commonly delineates objects easy of recognition. But the rock markings of the other type are quite different in appearance. They are characterized by grotesque figures, spiral and zigzag lines, etc., only seldom to be interpreted as reproductions of any object. ... These figures of apparently greater antiquity are generally found near the ruins, sometimes within the caves where the cliff-dwellings are situated. It therefore seems highly probable that the rock markings of this type are the work of the cliff dwellers."

Bill Howard

The Step House petroglyphs have stood the test of time; ancient symbols remain. The National Park Service removed more recent graffiti.

Mesa Verde National Park/Gustaf Nordenskiöld

Although the overall pace of geological change is slow, instantaneous changes sometimes occur. At Mesa Verde slabs of sandstone can separate and, within seconds, settle into
new positions. While such events are infrequent, two examples appear in the comparison of
today's photos with Nordenskiöld's. In this first view, the alcove with a structure is intact,
apparently undisturbed since its occupation.

Bill Howard

Here a rock slab has fallen from the roof of the alcove, demolishing a room.
Archaeologists have found evidence of similar rock falls in two other Mesa Verde sites while
they were occupied. They have speculated that the disaster caused the abandonment of
those sites.

Mesa Verde National Park/Gustaf Nordenskiöld

Kodak House, as it appeared in Nordenskiöld's day. This site was so named because it was where Gustaf stored his camera while he was away getting supplies.

1991

Bill Howard

Kodak House, as it was in 1991, looked much as it did a hundred years earlier. This photo was taken before the Wetherill Mesa fires that burned much of the vegetation on the mesa rim, greatly changing today's views.

Mesa Verde National Park/Gustaf Nordenskiöld

Two Wetherill brothers on horseback in Navajo Canyon on the Ute Mountain Reservation. Note the grazing cattle and the sparse vegetation.

Bill Howard

The same scene a century later. Without cattle grazing the land, the plant life is now far more luxuriant.

1891

Mesa Verde National Park/Gustaf Nordenskiöld

The second example of instantaneous change occurs near Echo House and the mesa above Navajo Canyon. In Nordenskiöld's photo the cliff face in the center of the picture, and the narrow ledge above it, show no breaks.

$$\boxed{1991}$$

Bill Howard

In comparing this view with Nordenskiöld's photo, it is evident that a large section is missing from the distant cliff face. A huge slab has detached and fallen, creating the beginning of an alcove. As the slab slid down, it also destroyed part of the narrow ridge at the top of the talus slope.

Epilogue

B etween July and October 1891, Gustaf Nordenskiöld devoted many arduous days to investigating, photographing, and mapping sites in an area that, 15 years later in 1906, would become Mesa Verde National Park. Neither he nor his friends, the Wetherills, could have imagined the far-reaching effect of his scientific work and the interest and attention publication of *The Cliff Dwellers of the Mesa Verde* would bring to the Four Corners area and the Southwest.

His trials did not end with the completion of his fieldwork in the Mesa Verde surrounds. On September 19, 1891, a front-page article appeared in the *Rocky Mountain News* detailing charges brought against Nordenskiöld. "Baron Lordenskiold [*sic*] Arrested, Charged with Devastating the Cliff Dwellings,"

Bill Howard

Square Tower House overlooking "penthouses" perched on the cliff.

the headline asserted. Nordenskiöld was arrested at midnight at Durango's Strater Hotel, by a United States deputy marshal. However, when he later appeared at U.S. District Court in Durango, all charges against him were dismissed. Correspondence from the Commissioner of Indian Affairs and Charles Bartholomew, U.S. Indian agent, and the Attorneys General of the United States and Colorado chronicles his arrest, charges of looting, bond posting, eventual release, and the apology for his detainment. Highly placed connections in Washington, D.C., at the Departments of State, Interior, and Justice, as well as at the Swedish consulate, and the intervention of the Swedish foreign minister helped resolve Nordenskiöld's case. After the charges were dismissed he no longer excavated, but spent time photographing and mapping the area in order to make an accurate historic and archaeological record of what he had seen.

Twenty-first century readers may question Nordenskiöld's seeming indifference to the effects his excavations and collections would have on contemporary Native Americans. His research at Mesa Verde occurred 15 years before the 1906 Antiquities Act and nearly a century prior to the 1990 enactment of the Native American Graves Protection and

Mesa Verde National Park

Anna Smitt and Gustaf Nordenskiöld

Repatriation Act (NAGPRA) which provides a process for the return of Native American cultural items including human remains, funerary objects, sacred objects, and items of "cultural patrimony to lineal descendants and culturally related Indian tribes."

Acowitz told Richard Wetherill there were ruins in Cliff Canyon and their Ute guide and co-worker certainly knew that the Wetherills and others were excavating. It would have been natural for Nordenskiöld to assume that Native Americans in the vicinity did not have strong objections to exploration of sites. Further, Nordenskiöld did obtain permits to explore on the Ute Mountain Reservation. He may have felt he had official approval for his activities.

Finally, viewed in the context of his time, his activities were consistent with contemporary practice. During the 19th and early 20th centuries archaeology burgeoned in many parts of the world. Egyptian tombs were excavated and remains of "lost" civilizations were found in Central America. In the best cases, it was common practice for discoverers to take whatever artifacts they wished for museums at home. In the worst cases, looters and pillagers traded in artifacts, finding lucrative markets among private collectors and foreign museums. At least Nordenskiöld was motivated by a desire to assemble a collection that could be publicly exhibited in Sweden. Many sites in and around Mesa Verde had already been ravaged by pot hunters by the time he arrived. We are fortunate today that he brought with him the knowledge and skills for proper excavation, documentation and photography.

Nordenskiöld's diaries and journals detail his outdoor experiences. For a young man suffering from consumption, his own accounts of physical activities belie his condition, as he scampered up cliffs and traversed precipices with apparent ease.

Nevertheless, Nordenskiöld's artifact collection and his intention to ship it to Europe concerned the citizens of Durango. Gustaf was perceived as a spoiled aristocrat, and some xenophobia may have underlain the charges as well, fueled by the image of a Viking looting ancient sites. With the exception of similar charges being brought against the Wetherills the following year, no Americans were prosecuted for removing artifacts, exploring sites on Ute lands or otherwise impacting prehistoric cultural remains in the Four Corners region until passage of the 1906 Antiquities Act. As had occurred with Nordenskiöld, the charges against the Wetherills also were dropped.

On November 4, 1891, Nordenskiöld was granted a permit to travel across the Navajo and Moqui [Hopi] reservations. Guided by Al Wetherill and a 20-year-old cowboy named Roe Ethridge, Gustaf left Mancos to study the people he believed to be modern descendants of Mesa Verde's ancestral residents and to explore the Grand Canyon. The "three tanned youths" with three pack horses, carrying provisions headed southwest on their way to the Grand Canyon. Along the way, they acquired a Navajo guide who led them toward the Lukachukai Mountains and on to Canyon de Chelly.

On November 16, they arrived at the Hopi villages of Hano and Walpi on First Mesa in time to attend a ceremonial dance. After trading provisions for textiles with the Hopi at Oraibi, they moved on to Tuba City, where they engaged the services of Seth Tanner, a Mormon guide, to show them the route to the Grand Canyon. Nordenskiöld's first view of the Canyon greatly impressed him. After an arduous descent of steep slopes, he and his companions were finally able to rest on the bank near the river slaking their thirst with the abundant waters of the Colorado River.

By December 2, the hardships of the trip had taken their toll. Nordenskiöld's journal describes a rag-tag band of three men riding "most sorry nags." Ascending the canyon, they encountered snowdrifts and thought about the journey that lay ahead as they turned toward Mancos. The travelers encountered freezing weather, snow, and fog along the way, barely managing to stay alive. But by December 21, the trail-weary bunch was back at the Wetherills' Alamo Ranch in Mancos.

Nordenskiöld returned to Sweden by spring 1892 and prepared his manuscript for *Cliff Dwellers of the Mesa Verde,* which was published the following year. He was invited to exhibit objects and photographs from his Mesa Verde collection at the Columbus jubilee in Madrid, Spain. The Queen of Spain awarded him the Order of Isabella Catolica in recognition of his exhibit as well as his exploration and contributions to understanding of the Americas. In December of that year he married Anna Rudolfina Smitt.

During the spring of 1894, Nordenskiöld caught a cold and became very ill. Nonetheless, he continued to correspond with his friends, the Wetherills, at Mesa Verde. In September a daughter was born to the young couple. Although he continued to work diligently at his mineralogical and photographic studies, Gustaf's health worsened. He asked to be taken to the mountains of Jamtland, but died en route. Only 26 years old at the time of his death, Gustaf Nordenskiöld was laid to rest in a churchyard near Vasterljunga, where members of his family are buried. On his gravestone is the Navajo whirling logs design.

In such a short life, Nordenskiöld accomplished much. It is nearly impossible to visit Mesa Verde National Park without hearing his name spoken by rangers, seeing it in the museum exhibits or reading it in books in the bookstore. The English translation of his *Cliff Dwellers of the Mesa Verde* has been reprinted many times since 1894 and is available in the park's bookstore today.

No recounting of Mesa Verde's early history would be complete without noting the enduring contribution to southwestern archaeology by Nordenskiöld's friends, guides, and mentors, the Wetherills. Fascination with pre-Columbian civilizations became the driving force in the lives of John, Richard, and Al Wetherill. No one who has sought out and visited southwestern sites can fail to be impressed by the extent of the Wetherills' explorations. It is a rare Four Corners prehistoric site that does not have evidence of Wetherill presence, whether on Mesa Verde, in Grand Gulch, at Navajo National Monument or elsewhere.

The Wetherill brothers realized their discoveries were scientifically and historically important. Two years before Nordenskiöld's visit, they had sought help from the leading archaeological authorities of the day. Their early letters to the Smithsonian and Peabody museums were quickly dismissed as if they came from rustic enthusiasts whose discoveries were not of major significance. Left to themselves, the Wetherills sought professional guidance wherever they could and welcomed all that Nordenskiöld taught them in their continuing effort to understand the ancients of the Southwest.

They continued a lively correspondence with Nordenskiöld for the rest of his short life. They were saddened to hear of the death of their friend and collaborator. Clearly, the friendship and respect the Wetherills and Gustaf had for each other were strong and surely would have endured had Nordenskiöld not died so young.

It would be many years before archaeologists finally recognized the merits of the Wetherills' work and even today some continue to underestimate the family's contributions to southwestern archaeology. Their affinity for Indians led three of the Wetherill brothers to become traders. John became an Indian agent on the Navajo Reservation and for more than 30 years served as caretaker of Navajo National Monument. The National Park

Service, in fact, describes him as the first "superintendent" of the monument. Richard was the agent for the Hyde Exploring Expedition that excavated Pueblo Bonito in Chaco Canyon, where he established a trading post.

Unfortunately, their preoccupation with sites led to the demise of the Alamo Ranch, which had to be sold in 1902. The brothers lie in widely separated graves: Richard was shot in a dispute near Chaco Canyon, New Mexico; John passed away in Arizona, on a train bound for California. Clayton is buried in Creede, Colorado, where he operated a fish hatchery, and Al died in Tulsa, Oklahoma.

The Wetherills tried to be good stewards of the antiquities they found. In today's context, however, they and all the other archaeologists of their day – including Gustaf Nordenskiöld – would, to varying degrees, be considered exploiters and despoilers of virgin prehistoric sites. As we have learned to tread much more lightly and to investigate much more carefully the legacy of the ancients, our ideas of proper respect for the past have changed significantly. Similarly, respect for the property and sensitivities of native peoples has changed as we learn from each other.

In 1906, Mesa Verde became a national park. That same year, the Antiquities Act became law, protecting historic and archaeological sites on government lands. All who enjoy visiting Mesa Verde today owe a great debt of thanks to Gustaf Nordenskiöld, who may have bent the rules by today's standards but, in doing so, made the first scientific record of this vast and beautiful southwestern legacy. His research and studies laid the groundwork for archaeological research that followed.

His early work established a baseline for those who followed. By photographing and documenting his work at Mesa Verde, Nordenskiöld provided indispensable pictures of the sites, landscape, and geography as they appeared before restoration and development. Gustaf Nordenskiöld was a blessing to future archaeologists and restoration professionals whose work is dedicated to understanding and preserving the wonders of the prehistoric past.

Re-photographing Nordenskiöld's original views provides a visual record of the effects of a time, nature, and human presence. In turn, a comparison of the photographs he took in 1891 with those taken a century later lends an appreciation of the forces that have wrought a century of change both great and small on the cultural remains and landscape of Mesa Verde National Park.

POSTSCRIPT
AND ACKNOWLEDGEMENTS

Kay Weber and Carol Ann Wetherill, descendents of Clayton Wetherill.

M esa Verde held a celebration in October 1991 to commemorate the 100th anniversary of Gustaf Nordenskiöld's visit to the Southwest. It was a gala occasion, celebrating the opening of new museum exhibits and offering people from the park, archaeology community, and the surrounding area an opportunity to gather and reflect on how much Mesa Verde had changed in 100 years of study and tourism development. As is often the case with such celebrations, the emphasis was on new facilities, artistry, and exhibits.

Those in attendance also represented a cross section reminiscent of the original participants in the early years of Mesa Verde's introduction to the world – Acowitz, the Wetherills, and Gustaf Nordenskiöld. All were honored for their ancestors' contributions to public recognition of Mesa Verde's importance as a prehistoric cultural site and thus its protection and preservation.

Several Wetherill relatives were present. Carol Ann Wetherill, Clayton's granddaughter, and Kay Weber, his great-granddaughter, were particularly helpful to us. Both still live in Southwest Colorado. We are grateful to them for sharing family stories and for leading us to Clayton's resting place in Creede.

Traditions run strong in some families, none more so than the Nordenskiöld clan. Gustaf Olaf Arrhenius also traveled from his home in San Diego to attend the 100th anniversary gala. The family name

From left: Shirley Hamilton, Doug Hamilton, Gustaf Olaf Arrhenius, who is Nordenskiöld's grandson, Bill Howard and Kathy Howard at the Nordenskiöld 100th Anniversary at Mesa Verde.

Kathy Howard

Arrhenius is familiar to all chemists (through Arrhenius's Law of the activation energy of chemical reactions), the result of work of Gustaf Olaf's forebears. As a world famous oceanographer at the Scripps Institution of Oceanography, Dr. Arrhenius is clearly continuing his family's tradition of scientific inquiry. In the context of Mesa Verde, however, he has an even closer connection. He is the grandson of Gustaf Nordenskiöld, born to the daughter who was no more than a baby when her father died.

Kathy Howard

Tommy May

The authors would have spent many days wandering in confusion through Mesa Verde country were it not for the friendship, hospitality and guidance of Don and Kathy Fiero, then Mesa Verde National Park's chief of interpretation and chief of stabilization, respectively. They were wonderful and patient hiking companions as we fiddled at length with tripods, bellows, and photographic plates.

Most of the sites Nordenskiöld photographed are in Mesa Verde National Park, but many lie outside in the adjacent Ute Mountain Tribal Park, an enterprise of the Ute Mountain Ute Tribe. Art Cuthair, park director, provided our introduction to these wonders. Tribal guide Tommy May was our "Acowitz," who took us to the sites and explained to us the Indian perspective of Mesa Verde.

Finally, all of us who were part of the Mesa Verde Project owe a great debt to our friend and enthusiastic supporter, Vic Goodwin, former proprietor of Vic's Photos in Cortez, Colorado. Vic has passed away and we miss him greatly. Many thanks, Vic, and may peace be with you!

Sources

Books
Arrhenius, Olaf W.: *Stones Speak and Waters Sing: The Life and Works of Gustaf Nordenskiold*, edited and annotated by Robert C. Lister and Florence C. Lister (Mesa Verde Museum Association, Inc., 1984).

Diamond, Irving L., and Olson, Daniel M., editors: *Letters of Gustaf Nordenskiöld Written in the Year 1891 and Articles from the Journals Ymer and Photographic Times.* Translated from Swedish by Daniel M. Olson (Mesa Verde Museum Association, Inc., 1991).

Fletcher, Maurine S., editor: *The Wetherills of the Mesa Verde: Autobiography of Benjamin Alfred Wetherill.* (Rutherford: Fairleigh Dickenson University Press, 1977).

McNitt, Frank: *Richard Wetherill: Anasazi – Pioneer Explorer of Ancient Ruins in the American Southwest* (University of New Mexico Press, 1957).

Nordenskiöld, Gustaf: *The Cliff Dwellers of the Mesa Verde – Southwestern Colorado: Their Pottery and Implements.* Translated by D. Lloyd Morgan (The Rio Grande Press, Second Printing, 1980 – reprint of 1893 edition published by P. A. Norstedt & Söner, Stockholm. Translation of *Ruiner af klippboningar i Mesa Verde's cañons*).

Brochures
"Cliff Dweller Exhibit – World's Columbian Exposition," (Chicago: H. Jay Smith Exploring Company, 1893) Testimonials from visitors including H.R.H. The Infanta Eulalia of Spain touted the interesting display. Howard Collection.

"The Cliff Dwellers: The World's Greatest Historical Ethnological and Educational Exhibition – on the Pike," W. Maurice Tobin, Manager. Stereoviews of the 1893 exhibit show the towering faux cliff dwelling with trails to the top which visitors could climb. No. 8559. Home of the Cliff Dwellers, World's Columbian Exposition. (Copyright 1894, B.W. Kilburn). Howard Collection.

Periodicals
The Rocky Mountain News, Denver, Colorado, Saturday, September 19, 1891, page 1.

Harrell, David: " 'We contacted Smithsonian:' The Wetherills at Mesa Verde," *New Mexico Historical Review.* Vol. 62, No. 3, July 1987. pp. 229 – 248.

Other

Chas. A. Bartholomew, Indian Agent, Southern Ute Agency to Commissioner of Indian Affairs. National Archives, RG 75 Registers of Letters Received 1881 - 1907. Roll 48, Vol. 174. September 19, 1891. No. 34822. Also October 7, 1891, No. 36635. Chas. A. Bartholomew to Baron Nordenskiöld, October 7, 1891, No. 35513. Attorney General to Commissioner of Indian Affairs, October 12, 1891, A.G. No. 9512-1891.

Geo. Handler, Acting Secretary, Department of the Interior to the Commissioner of Indian Affairs. Office of Indian Affairs, November 4, 1891. No. 40093.

Ronald F. Lee, Special Assistant to the Director, National Park Service. *The Antiquities Act of 1906.* Office of History and Historic Architecture, Eastern Service Center, Washington, D.C., November 16, 1970.

Personal correspondence Carol Ann Wetherill to Kathleen L. Howard. (Monte Vista, Colorado, July 24, 1992, and Creede, Colorado, July 27, 1992). Correspondence in author's collection.

Private conversation with Linda Martin, Mesa Verde National Park.

INDEX

V-Y